THE WILD WEST

Mike Stotter

KINGFISHER

KINGFISHER BOOKS
An imprint of Larousse plc
New Penderel House, 283-288 High Holborn
London WC1V 7HZ

First published by Kingfisher 1997
10 9 8 7 6 5 4 3 2

Copyright © Larousse plc 1997

A CIP catalogue record for this book is available from the British
Library.

ISBN 0 7534 0107 X

Editor: Clare Oliver
Design: Ben White Associates and Terry Woodley
Cover design: Terry Woodley
Cover illustration: Kenny McKendry (Artist Partners)
Art editor: Christina Fraser
Picture research: Veneta Bullen
Printed in Italy

CONTENTS

THE AUTHOR

Mike Stotter has long been fascinated by the Wild
West. To date, his books have been mostly fictional –
he has written six pulp Western novels. He has also
contributed to *Twentieth Century Western Writers* and
the *Encyclopedia of Frontier and Western Fiction*. He
and his family have settled some way east of the
frontier, in Essex.

THE CONSULTANT

Dee Brown is a leading expert on the American West.
He is most renowned for *Bury My Heart at Wounded
Knee*, which has sold more than five million copies
worldwide. He has written more than 20 works of
fiction and non-fiction relating to American frontier
history. He lives with his wife in Little Rock, Arkansas.

EARLY DAYS

American Indians lived undisturbed throughout North and South America until the European discovery of the 'New World' in 1492. Now the nations of Europe raced to claim the rich 'new' land for themselves. But it was the Spanish *conquistadores* (conquerors) who had the greatest impact on the native people.

The king of Spain was determined to find the legendary 'Seven Cities of Gold'. To the Southwest came Francisco Vásquez de Coronado and to the East, Hernando de Soto. Despite vast armies of men and animals, neither man found the mythical treasure.

The Spanish treated the Pueblo Indians of New Mexico very harshly. In 1680 the Indians fought back, killing almost 400 Spaniards and stealing their horses. Until then, dogs were used to carry heavy loads but now horses, called 'big dogs', took their place. Within one hundred years, most tribes had horses. On horseback, they could hunt farther afield.

What the Spaniards couldn't get through trade, they took by force. Unco-operative villages were attacked and plundered. The defenders' arrows, lances and war clubs were no match for the invaders' rifles and steel swords. The *conquistadores* enslaved the men and boys and took the women as cooks and servants.

▼ In 1783, colonists in the East declared their independence from Britain, and the United States was formed. But up until the early 1800s, vast areas of the continent remained colonies, belonging to Spain, France and Britain. Gradually, the United States started to expand its boundaries. Sometimes it fought for territory, as it did with Britain in 1812. It also bought land. In 1803, Napoleon sold Louisiana to the United States for $15 million.

BRITISH (until 1818)

FRENCH (The Louisiana Purchase 1803)

SPANISH (Mexican after 1823)

THE UNITED STATES 1783

N

0 MILES 500
0 KM 800

KEY TO STATES WITH DATES THEY JOINED THE UNION
1 Michigan 1837
2 Illinois 1818
3 Indiana 1816
4 Ohio 1803
5 Vermont 1791
6 Maine 1820
7 Missouri 1821
8 Kentucky 1792
9 Arkansas 1836
10 Tennessee 1796
11 Louisiana 1812
12 Mississippi 1817
13 Alabama 1819
14 Florida 1819

The wild frontier

In 1803, President Jefferson bought the Louisiana Territory from France. The land stretched all the way from the Mississippi River to the eastern slopes of the Rocky Mountains. Expeditions set out to map the West. Many of the early explorers, such as Zebulon Pike, Jim Bridger and Thomas 'Brokenhand' Fitzpatrick, became the first settlers of the wild frontier, trapping furs in the mountains for their living. The West captured the imagination as a place of opportunity, freedom and rich land; the rush to settle the West had begun.

Early explorers

Meriwether Lewis and William Clark captained the president's Corps of Discovery – the expedition to explore the new territory and reach the Pacific coast. They took three boats laden with gifts and trading goods, and 30 men. Clark brought along his black slave, York. They also hired a young Shoshoni woman, called Sacajawea, to be their guide. The expedition took over a year, crossing the Rockies along the Oregon Trail, and reaching the coast in 1805.

Mountain man of legend

James 'Tomahawk' Beckwourth headed west from Virginia in 1826. There, he met a Crow woman who claimed he was her long lost son, and called him Morning Star. The tribe adopted him and he fought alongside Crow warriors against the Blackfeet. He became a war chief and he was even married to a chief's two daughters at the same time. He later worked as a government guide and interpreter. He found a route through the Sierra Nevada Mountains to California, and it was named the Beckwourth Pass after him.

▶ **Fall of the Alamo,** by Robert Onderdonk

▲ In the early 1830s Texas was under Mexican control. A small Spanish mission and fortress called The Alamo was the site of a bloody 12-day siege in 1836. All 182 Texan defenders, including the famous Davy Crockett, Jim Bowie and Colonel William Travis, were massacred by 3,000 Mexican troops. But just six weeks later, Texas finally won its independence with the stirring battle cry of 'Remember the Alamo!'. In 1845 Texas joined the Union and became the 28th American state. This new land continued the westward expansion of American control. And because of the large herds of cattle there, Texas was settled by ranchers and cowboys and became a vital part of the West's cattle industry.

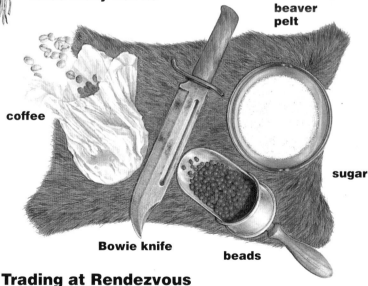

beaver pelt

coffee

Bowie knife

beads

sugar

Trading at Rendezvous

After lonely trapping in the wilds, the highlight of a mountain man's year was the month-long meeting called Rendezvous. He traded his furs for knives, sugar and gunpowder. But best of all there was plenty of whiskey, gambling and horse-racing!

Clues to the past

The true days of the Wild West began with the Louisiana Purchase in 1803 and came to an end in 1890. Paintings, photographs, diaries, letters, newspapers and American Indian artefacts surviving from that time allow historians to build up a picture of how the people of the West lived – and died.

▶ *The Cowboy,* by Frederic Remington

◀ If you couldn't write down words, how would you keep a record of your family history or honour a dead chief? Totem poles are found mainly in the far Northwest of the United States. Some tell of a tribe's ancestors; 'shame poles' were built to disgrace people; others were like upright coffins, containing a dead body. Like this Kwakiutl totem pole, many still stand today and they tell us a lot about the way of life of the American Indians who carved and painted them.

AMERICAN INDIAN ARTEFACTS
1 Ice Age stone weapon point, found at Folsom, New Mexico
2 Chipewyan caribou bone scraper
3 Papago pot
4 Ute moccasins
5 Potawatomi pipe
6 Pima coiled basket
7 Naiche painting on doeskin
8 Navajo blanket
9 Iroquois carved antler comb

Photography

The first photograph was taken in 1826 and the time of the Wild West is one of the earliest in history to be recorded by photos. Pictures have survived of everything, from the unspoilt landscapes to the characters who lived there – cowboys, settlers, gold-miners and American Indians.

On canvas

Painters George Catlin, Karl Bodmer, Mary Foote and Albert Bierstadt knew that they had to capture the Wild West before it vanished forever. Frederic Remington and Charles Russell rode alongside cowboys and soldiers, recording what they saw in beautiful paintings.

▼ Using wool from their own sheep, Navajo women wove these colourful, patterned blankets so tight that they were almost waterproof. Even the smallest took weeks to complete.

The written word

Ordinary diaries, like that of Susan Shelby Magoffin, were simple accounts of everyday experiences. Many early settlers wrote private diaries which were later published. Accounts of frontier life by famous explorers sold in huge numbers at the time, to readers eager for excitement. Guidebooks are also a valuable source of first-hand information; they were written to let a settler know what to expect and to describe the conditions on a wagon train.

Susan Shelby Magoffin

In a typical Dakota (or Sioux) village on the plains, a stream provided water, cottonwood trees supplied firewood, young spring grass fed the horses and there was plenty of open space to pitch the tepees.

It took up to 12 buffalo hides to make a family tepee. It was the women who made, owned and erected the tepees, stretching the hides over pine poles. A fire inside kept everyone warm in winter, while in summer the sides were lifted to let the breeze in.

Games were enjoyed by old and young alike. Men and boys played stickball, which was known as 'little brother of war' because many ended up with cuts or even broken bones! Horse races were popular, too, and men liked to gamble with stones and straws.

▶ Only the women made clothes. The buffalo skin was pegged out, scraped free of flesh, then washed with water and grease. Once cleaned, the skin was left to dry in the sun. Then the women rubbed it for days until it was soft and pliable.

TEPEE LIFE

Each American Indian tribe had its own way of life, suited to its surroundings. But all tribes had a similar social structure. The three most important men were the chief, the medicine man and the war chief. Next came the elders and warriors, then the squaws and children. Like other Plains Indians, the Dakota (or Sioux) lived in villages. Life was hard. Those children who survived were cared for by all the members of the tribe. They had toys, games and pet puppies. Boys practised with bows and arrows. Dolls were popular with the girls, who learned the skills they'd need for adult life from their mothers.

▲ To make pemmican, cut buffalo meat into narrow strips and dry slowly over a fire or in the sun. Pound this 'jerky' and mix with chokecherries and buffalo fat. Stored in sacks, this food can keep for five years.

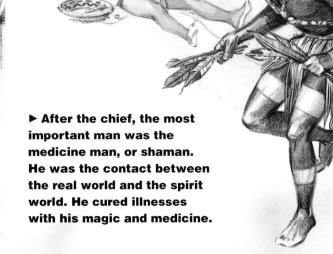

▶ After the chief, the most important man was the medicine man, or shaman. He was the contact between the real world and the spirit world. He cured illnesses with his magic and medicine.

11

Homes of the brave

**Tlingit
(Northwest Coast)**

With the coming of the horse, it was much easier for American Indians to move about freely. They often moved with the seasons. Some tribes, such as the Arapaho, followed the migrating buffalo. They spent the hot summer months in the cool north and moved south as it grew colder.

Almost half of the North American Indian tribes were based between the Mississippi River and the Rocky Mountains. But tribes were often forced out of their original homelands, either by settlers or by other jealous tribes. The eastern tribes were the first to obtain guns. They used them to push other tribes west and steal their land.

Who lived where?

Tribes are sometimes grouped together by area. The four western areas are the Southwest, Plains, Northwest Coast and California-Intermountain. The other, non-western areas are the Far North, Caribbean, Middle American and Eastern Woodlands.

**Hupa
(California-Intermountain)**

Western tribes

Frontiersmen and pioneers encountered many different tribes in the Wild West. Each was distinct and usually had its own language. Many tribes named themselves after their holy ancestors. These spiritual guardians were known as the 'totem' and often took the form of an animal.

**Pawnee
(Plains)**

Types of dwelling

Depending on what building material was to hand, different tribes had different types of houses. Pueblos (1) were built from adobe bricks, tepees (2) from hides, wigwams (3) of bark and leaves, and lodges (4) from earth and wood.

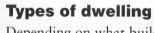

**Navajo
(Southwest)**

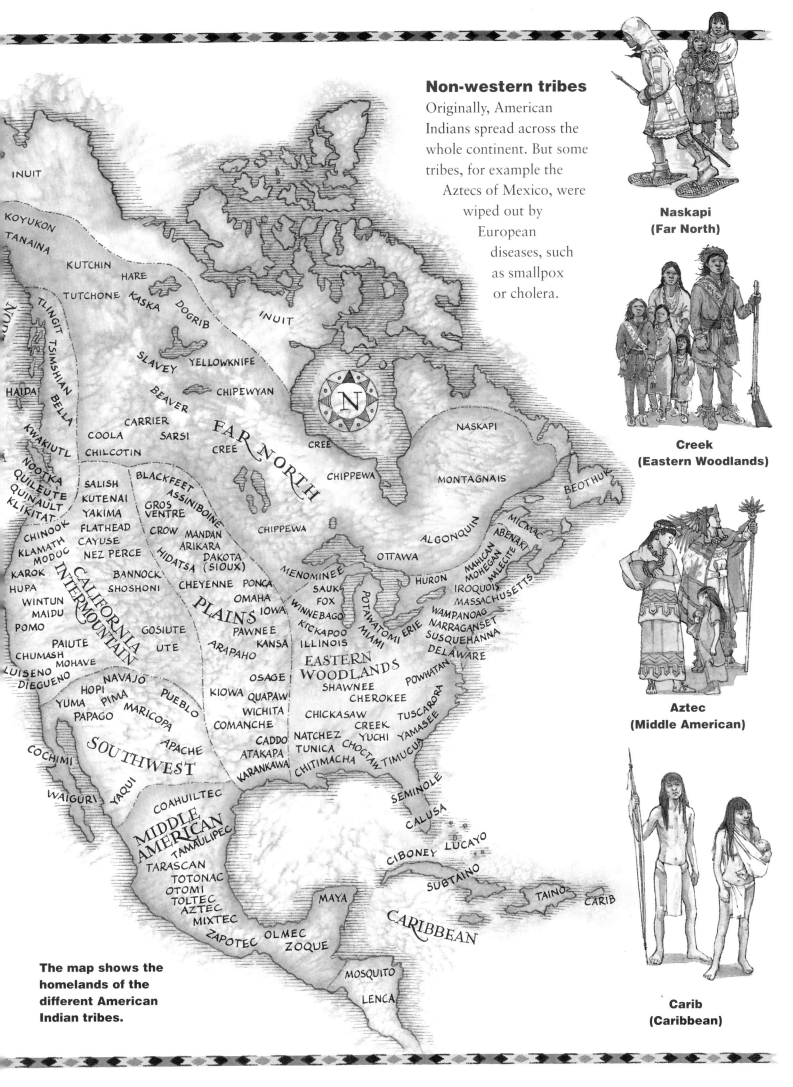

Non-western tribes

Originally, American Indians spread across the whole continent. But some tribes, for example the Aztecs of Mexico, were wiped out by European diseases, such as smallpox or cholera.

Naskapi (Far North)

Creek (Eastern Woodlands)

Aztec (Middle American)

Carib (Caribbean)

INUIT

KOYUKON
TANAINA
KUTCHIN
HARE
TUTCHONE KASKA
TLINGIT
TSIMSHIAN
DOGRIB
INUIT
SLAVEY YELLOWKNIFE
HAIDA
BELLA
BEAVER CHIPEWYAN
KWAKIUTL
CARRIER
COOLA SARSI
NOOTKA
QUILEUTE
QUINAULT
CHILCOTIN
CREE
FAR NORTH
NASKAPI
KLIKITAT
CREE
CREE
BEOTHUK
SALISH BLACKFEET
CHINOOK
KUTENAI
ASSINIBOINE
MONTAGNAIS
KLAMATH
YAKIMA
GROS
VENTRE
CHIPPEWA
ALGONQUIN
MICMAC
MODOC
FLATHEAD
CROW MANDAN
ABENAKI
KAROK
CAYUSE
ARIKARA
MAHICAN
MALECITE
HUPA
NEZ PERCE
HIDATSA
DAKOTA
(SIOUX)
OTTAWA
MOHEGAN
WINTUN
BANNOCK
CHEYENNE PONCA
MENOMINEE
HURON
IROQUOIS
MASSACHUSETTS
MAIDU
SHOSHONI
OMAHA
SAUK
WAMPANOAG
POMO
GOSIUTE
IOWA
FOX
NARRAGANSET
PAIUTE
UTE
PAWNEE
WINNEBAGO
POTAWATOMI ERIE
SUSQUEHANNA
CHUMASH
ARAPAHO
KANSA
KICKAPOO
MIAMI
DELAWARE
MOHAVE
ILLINOIS
LUISENO
EASTERN
POWHATAN
DIEGUENO
OSAGE
WOODLANDS
CALIFORNIA INTERMOUNTAIN
NAVAJO
KIOWA QUAPAW
SHAWNEE
HOPI
PUEBLO
WICHITA
CHEROKEE
YUMA PIMA
COMANCHE
CHICKASAW
TUSCARORA
PAPAGO MARICOPA
CADDO
NATCHEZ
CREEK YUCHI YAMASEE
APACHE
ATAKAPA
TUNICA CHOCTAW TIMUCUA
SOUTHWEST
KARANKAWA
CHITIMACHA
COCHIMI
YAQUI
SEMINOLE
WAIGURI
COAHUILTEC
CALUSA
MIDDLE
AMERICAN
TAMAULIPEC
LUCAYO
TARASCAN
CIBONEY
TOTONAC
SUBTAINO
OTOMI
TOLTEC
MAYA
TAINO CARIB
AZTEC
MIXTEC
ZAPOTEC OLMEC
CARIBBEAN
ZOQUE

MOSQUITO
LENCA

The map shows the homelands of the different American Indian tribes.

13

Hunting and food

Some tribes were hunters, relying on buffalo and other game for food, shelter and clothing. Most American Indians gathered foods from the wild, too. Tribes such as the Mandans, who lived in areas of good soil, were excellent farmers. In fact, 60 percent of the crops we grow today come from plants first cultivated by the American Indians. They include corn, beans, tomatoes, squash, potatoes, chilli peppers and vanilla. Not all crops provided food – there were medicinal herbs, tobacco, cotton, and plants for vegetable dyes.

Using the buffalo

Every part of the buffalo was used. The meat fed the family, while soap made from the fat kept them clean. Bones were carved into tools and knives, and the hide made clothing, tepees and shields. Thick buffalo hair was woven into rope or used for children's toys.

BUFFALO PRODUCTS
1 sacred decorated skull
2 toy made of buffalo hair
3 leather war shield
4 pemmican hammer of leather and bone
5 buffalo-skin blanket

The buffalo runners

Before the days of rifles, hunting buffalo was a dangerous business. A hunter would ride in close, select one buffalo, and herd it away from the others. A team of skilled hunters could kill a small herd in about 15 minutes, but if they weren't careful, they could be thrown from their horses and be stampeded to death by the panicking animals.

Preparing the corn

Corn was part of the American Indian's staple diet. Women ground the kernels into flour between two stones. To make corn fritters, water was added to the flour, the cakes were fried in a skillet over the fire.

Tasty harvest

Corn (1), beans and squash (2) were the three main crops and were often called the Trinity. Women grew them in their own gardens. Sunflowers (3) were grown, too, for their nutritious seeds, and rice (4) was gathered from the wild. Vanilla pods and wild berries (5) were used in cooking and preserving.

The wolf headdress shows this warrior is a scout.

A horse's war paint showed how many raids it had made.

coup stick

CHEYENNE WARRIOR

1

What's your name?

Some children had no name until they were teenagers. Like many, the Apache chief Black Eagle got his through a vision (1). He earned his name by taking part in a horse-stealing raid, where he saw the eagle from his dream (2). Black Eagle went on to become chief of his tribe (3).

Warriors

Not only did tribes fight the settlers and soldiers, they warred amongst themselves to gain new territory and to prove their courage. The Dakota were great enemies of the Crow and Pawnees. The Comanche were swift and ferocious on horseback, and everyone feared the Apaches. Eagle-feather headdresses, known as 'war bonnets', were worn only by those who earned them by their acts of bravery. Others wore simple headbands or skullcaps.

◄ Warriors would kill or even scalp the enemy, but one of the most respected war deeds was 'counting coup' – touching the enemy but not killing him. The more coups counted, the greater a man's status as a warrior. Many used a special, curved stick, called a coup stick, which was decorated with eagle feathers.

2

3

Dressed to kill

In addition to their head-dresses, which showed their position within their tribe's warrior society, warriors wore war paint for spiritual protection. Comanches used black and white; Crows had red-striped faces for horse-stealing raids; and Blackfeet painted a white line across the face for vengeance.

Comanche

Crow

Weapons of war

An elk-horn bow could fire fatal arrows over a short range, but for closer combat a warrior favoured a tomahawk or war club. Lances were thrust forwards to dismount or gut an enemy rider. Most warriors also carried a shield for protection.

shield

tomahawk

war club

quiver holding bow and arrows

war lance

Blackfeet

The warrior society was a kind of club that selected men of the tribe belonged to. In battle the warriors followed the war chief, a man picked for his leadership and fighting skills. In peacetime the warriors acted as the tribe's police force. They were known for their discipline and fierceness. Loyalty to their tribe and their society was to the death.

The Sun Dance ceremony

A warrior committed himself to his tribe by taking part in a religious ceremony called the Sun Dance. For eight days he had no food or drink and gazed straight into the Sun. He wore body paint and his chest was pierced with skewers, tied by thongs to a sacred pole. He danced and jerked until the flesh gave way, leaving scars which he wore with pride.

Religion and myth

To every American Indian, the land and the spirit life were the most important matters in the world. All tribes believed in a spiritual force that was in the earth, animals, the sky and everything around them. They paid their respect in rituals and ceremonies, some adopting elements from Christianity brought by the Spanish.

A young girl's vigil

Every young teenager performed a vigil as part of their journey into adulthood. Catherine Wabose became her tribe's prophetess after her vigil. Following a six-day fast, she heard a supernatural voice tell her to walk along a shining path. First she met 'Everlasting Standing Woman', then 'Little Man Spirit' who said his name would be her first son's name. 'Bright Blue Sky' gave her the gift of life. Finally she received the gift of prophecy.

Sweat it out

Though it varied from tribe to tribe, the sweat lodge ceremony was universal among American Indians. It was used to purify the soul or heal sickness. The sweat lodge was dome-shaped, built with saplings and covered with blankets or hide. It seated about six people. A leader in charge of the ceremony threw herbs and water over the heated stones in a firepit which gave off purifying steam. The participants sat in the lodge chanting and praying to the spirits.

Many dances, prayers and ceremonies were performed for special occasions. An American Indian's life – and death – was spent trying to please the spirits. Tribes such as the Dakota built tall platforms on which they placed their dead, to bring them closer to the sky. So that a tribe's history was not forgotten, mythical stories were handed down by word of mouth from generation to generation.

The Ghost Dance

The Ghost Dance was practised by Indians of the Plains and Great Basin. A Paiute prophet named Wovoka told his ghost dancers that praying, chanting and dancing in circles for days would bring back dead relatives, the buffalo, and even return the land to the way it had been before Europeans came. The ghost dancers wore shirts covered in symbols which were said to protect them from harm.

RANCHES & RANCHERS

The Spanish brought over the first cattle. After Texan independence, millions of longhorns were left roaming free. Young men went to make their fortunes by rounding up and claiming the wild herds as their own.

Springtime round-up

In spring, the cattle were driven down from their winter pasture into corrals. Riders would rope the new calves and drag them to the branding crew. The red-hot iron marked the calves with their owner's brand for life.

Line riders

The first ranches had no fences. Their boundaries were natural barriers, such as rivers. Line riders worked the remotest parts of the ranch making sure the cattle stayed on their side of the range, or line.

Food for all

Out in the middle of nowhere, a ranch had to be self-sufficient. Milk came from the dairy cows, eggs from the hen-house, and water from a stream or well. Meat was plentiful and a small kitchen garden supplied fresh vegetables.

Who's in charge?

When a ranch owner was away on business, the foreman was in charge. He hired and fired everyone from the cook, to the cowboys, wranglers and bronc-busters.

There was plenty of free grass and good water in the West – important ingredients for fattening cows. Cowboys drove the cattle to the nearest cow town, and from there the animals were carried east by train. Demand grew and 'cattle barons' grew rich. Charles Goodnight was one of the best-known barons – he's also famous for inventing the chuck wagon so his cowboys could eat well on the trail. John and Elizabeth Iliff supplied beef to the Union Pacific Railroad, buying up to 15,000 steers a year.

Charles Goodnight

Elizabeth Iliff

Brands

The best way to know who owned a steer was to read its brand. It was finders keepers if you found an orphaned calf with no brand (known as a maverick). Anyone could claim the unmarked calf and brand it as his own.

Richard King's running W

Mifflin Kenedy's laurel leaf

rocking chair

hog eye

broken arrow

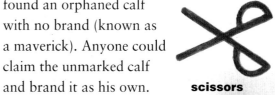

scissors

pipe

A cowboy and his horse

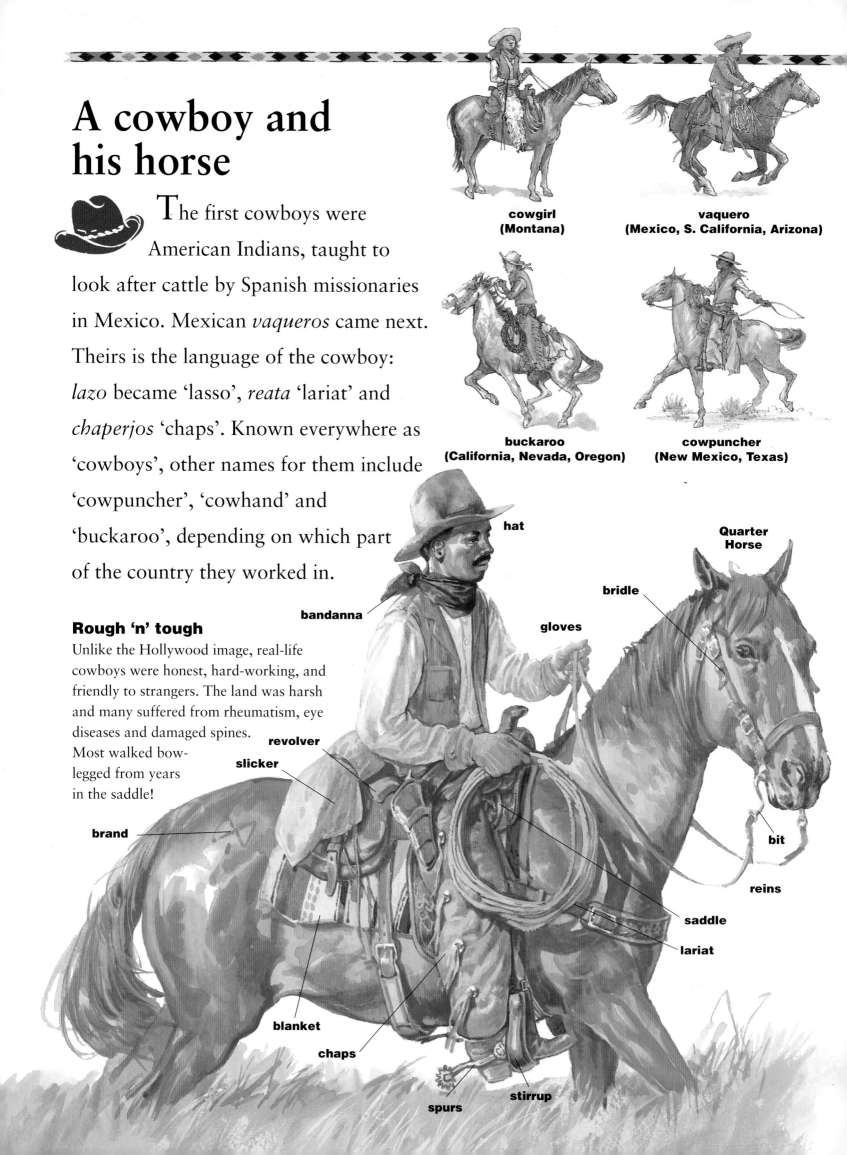

The first cowboys were American Indians, taught to look after cattle by Spanish missionaries in Mexico. Mexican *vaqueros* came next. Theirs is the language of the cowboy: *lazo* became 'lasso', *reata* 'lariat' and *chaperjos* 'chaps'. Known everywhere as 'cowboys', other names for them include 'cowpuncher', 'cowhand' and 'buckaroo', depending on which part of the country they worked in.

Rough 'n' tough

Unlike the Hollywood image, real-life cowboys were honest, hard-working, and friendly to strangers. The land was harsh and many suffered from rheumatism, eye diseases and damaged spines. Most walked bow-legged from years in the saddle!

cowgirl
(Montana)

vaquero
(Mexico, S. California, Arizona)

buckaroo
(California, Nevada, Oregon)

cowpuncher
(New Mexico, Texas)

hat

Quarter
Horse

bridle

gloves

bandanna

revolver

slicker

brand

bit

reins

saddle

lariat

blanket

chaps

stirrup

spurs

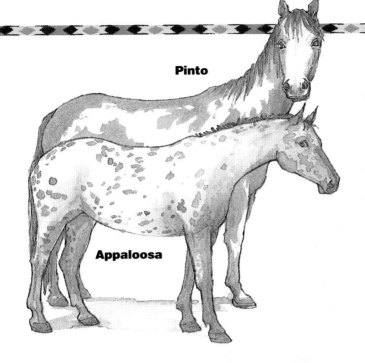

Pinto

Appaloosa

A cowboy chose a horse suited to the job and found a gelding more reliable than a mare. The strong, agile Quarter Horse was the most popular breed with cowboys. But some selected a horse for its looks, such as the Appaloosa, favourite of the Nez Percé Indians, or the dappled Pinto.

Spurs & saddles

Often called 'gentle persuaders', spurs were used to control a horse. Sharp new spurs had the points blunted. There were two main styles of saddle, the Texas (1) and the California (2). A saddle lasted a lifetime and there was an old cowboy saying that 'to sell your saddle' meant you were broke.

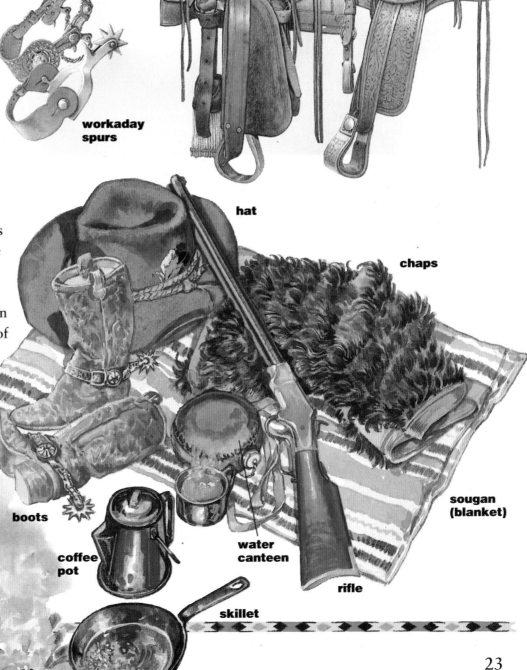

fancy spurs

workaday spurs

hat

chaps

boots

coffee pot

water canteen

rifle

sougan (blanket)

skillet

Cowboy gear

The cowboy's leather boots were handmade. Five-centimetre high heels prevented the foot slipping out of the stirrup. The cowboy's hat, often a Stetson, had a broad brim to shade the eyes from the sun and a tall crown to keep the head cool. Chaps, made of either leather or wool, were worn over jeans to protect the legs from thorns or prickly cacti. Having water could make the difference between life or death, so the cowboy kept his canteen full and close to hand. A sougan, or quilted blanket, kept him warm at night. The cowboy's rifle was used for hunting and protection. So he wasn't hampered on horseback, the cowboy's rifle and bed roll were carried in the chuck wagon.

On the trail

On a cattle drive, there was one cowboy to every 250 cattle. A 2,000 kilometre long drive took about four months and, on average, the cowboy earnt $30 per month. The trail boss headed the column, which could be as wide as 3 kilometres. At the sides, flank riders stopped the steers wandering away, while at the back the drag riders pushed them forwards.

Life on the trail

Up an hour before dawn, a cowboy spent up to 14 hours in the saddle every day. The men took turns keeping watch at night.

Danger!

River crossings were a hazardous time, as many of the cowboys couldn't swim. It didn't take much to stampede nervous cattle. Thunderstorms, grass fires, even a cowboy sneezing could set them running!

flank riders

chuck wagon

trail boss

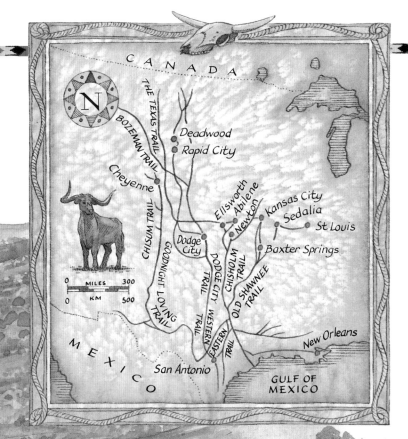

Cattle-trail blazers

The cattle routes had to be carved out of the harsh terrain. Rancher Charles Goodnight and his partner Oliver Loving founded the Goodnight-Loving Trail; Joseph McCoy's route used part of the Chisholm Trail; Granville Stuart drove his steers across Oregon to Montana; and Lucien Maxwell cut a new route to Nebraska called the Western Trail.

humped Brahman

Texas longhorn

Hereford

British shorthorn

drag riders

Breeds of cow

'Critters', 'beeves' or 'dogies' were the cowboys' favourite nicknames for cattle. The Texas longhorn was the predominant cow in the Southwest. Later, the shorthorn, the Hereford and the humped Brahman were introduced. They provided better meat and were immune to 'Texas tick'.

Campfire songs

A sweet-singing cowboy entertained the men and calmed the cattle. There were rousing trail-driving songs, like *The Old Chisholm Trail*, as well as gentle lullabies.

The Night Herding Song

Oh say, little dogies, when you goin' to lay down, and give up this driftin' and rovin' around?

My horse is leg-weary and I'm awful tired, but if you get away, I'm sure to be fired.

Lay down, little dogies, lay down, hi-o, hi-o, hi-o.

▲ The chuck wagon and campfire were a focal point on the drive. Bacon, bread and beans were usually on the menu, but dried and canned food helped vary the meals. Strong black coffee was a must with every meal.

Cow towns

After long months on the trail, the cowboy hit town. After a quick bath and shave, he threw away his old, torn jeans and put on his new 'store-boughts'. Then he headed for the nearest saloon. His favourite drinks were whiskey and beer. On a drunken spree, the cowboy often terrorized the ordinary town citizens. Forget the fist fights in the movies – 'manstoppers' (guns) and knives were the norm. More often than not, a cowboy headed back to camp with an empty wallet and a sore head!

Hitting the saloon
Whether it was a tent, a Mexican *cantina* or a saloon, the bar was a place where men could relax, have a drink and a meal, play cards or listen to music. Lonesome cowboys could pay a dollar to dance with a girl. Many saloons became famous, such as The Bucket of Blood Saloon, The Jersey Lilly and The Occidental.

In the bar
The bar took up a lot of space and was well-stocked with bottled wines, whiskey and other spirits. There was home-brewed beer, as well as imported ale from England and stout from Ireland. The saloon also sold home-baked food and luxuries such as pickled eggs or cheese.

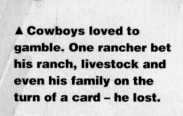
▲ Cowboys loved to gamble. One rancher bet his ranch, livestock and even his family on the turn of a card – he lost.

Horsin' around

Cowboys were noted for bad behaviour when they hit town. After months of hard work, they let off steam. The sheriff would lock up a drunken cowboy causing trouble, and not let him out till he was sober.

▲ *In Without Knocking*, by Charles Russell

While stock buyers and cattlemen frequented fancy hotel bars, cowboys went to the cheaper saloons. Hispanic and black cowboys were often forced to drink in separate saloons. Cow towns attracted all sorts: gunmen, outlaws, thieves and gamblers. The Kansas cow town of Abilene employed respected lawmen, such as Wild Bill Hickok and Bat Masterson, to keep the peace.

▼ The cow town was the place where the trail met the railroad. Towns like Wichita, Ellsworth and Abilene flourished because of the cattle business. Stock buyers came from the East to buy whole herds to load on trains for New York and Chicago.

◄ To increase profits, bar owners used to employ female singers. They were accompanied by a pianist, violinist or banjo player. Some put on a whole night of theatrical acts with jugglers and knife throwers.

WESTWARD HO!

Between 1836 and 1890 nearly 750,000 people crossed the western frontier. They came from all over the world, lured by the promise of land and a better future. The Mormons headed west to escape persecution and find their own 'promised land'. They settled near the Great Salt Lake in Utah in June 1847. And, when gold was discovered in California in 1848, it sparked a rush of fortune-seekers.

Westward trails

With no highways to get from place to place, American Indians and Spanish adventurers had to find their own way. Later, explorers and traders followed the same routes. Settlers' wagons widened them into dusty trails. These formed a vast network across the prairies, deserts and mountains of the West.

The trip from Independence to Oregon City covered 3,700 km and took six months. Pioneers said: "The weak died on the way and courage never left."

There wasn't room on the wagon for everyone and many made the long journey on foot. Wagons often broke down and heavy furniture was discarded along the way to lighten the load.

Heading into unknown land had its dangers. Death by drowning, cholera, smallpox or accidental shootings was all too common. Many babies and young children didn't finish the trip. Livestock died from exhaustion or from eating poisonous plants. Hostile American Indians would often steal cattle, oxen and horses.

Stocking a Conestoga wagon didn't come cheap. Buying enough farm tools, furniture, food and clothing for a family of up to 16 could cost an incredible $1,500 – almost five years' wages!

Staking a claim

At their journey's end, pioneers claimed their land by putting up a marker. The Homestead Act of 1862 allowed a settler 65 hectares of land for just $10 – so long as he stayed and improved the land for at least five years.

Making a home

Early pioneers built their homes with whatever nature provided. Log cabins were built in the forests of the Northwest. On the plains there were few trees, so cave-like homes were dug into the sides of hills. These tended to collapse, so sod houses took their place. When they could afford to, settlers replaced these with more permanent structures.

A soddy

It took 4,000 square metres of turf to cut enough bricks to build a sod house or 'soddy'. The owners were nicknamed sodbusters.

Doors and windows

Doors were made from packing cases. Greased paper kept out the wind until the settlers could afford glass windows.

Soddy life

Nature played havoc with sodbusters. Droughts were common. In a summer storm, bolts of lightning might set the prairies on fire. There were destructive twisters and dust storms. Plagues of locusts ate all the crops. In winter, blizzards froze the earth and the people.

Keeping warm

On the treeless plains there were no logs to use as fuel for cooking and heating. Sunflowers and greasewood were burned instead, but more often buffalo or cow dung, known as 'chips', was gathered. It made the house smelly but at least everyone was warm!

It was hard work growing up in a pioneer family. Young children had to milk the cows, feed the chickens and tend the horses. The lucky ones attended school, with children of all ages in the one class – but they still had to do their chores. Illness and disease struck many families. Cholera and smallpox were killers. The nearest doctor might live many kilometres away, so the pioneers treated themselves with home-made remedies.

▲ Though work was shared around, women did the cooking, cleaning, and washing as well as helping with the crops and animals.

Water for life

Homesteaders couldn't survive without water. Some relied on a nearby river or creek, or collected rainwater in barrels. Others dug wells or used windmills to pump water up out of the ground.

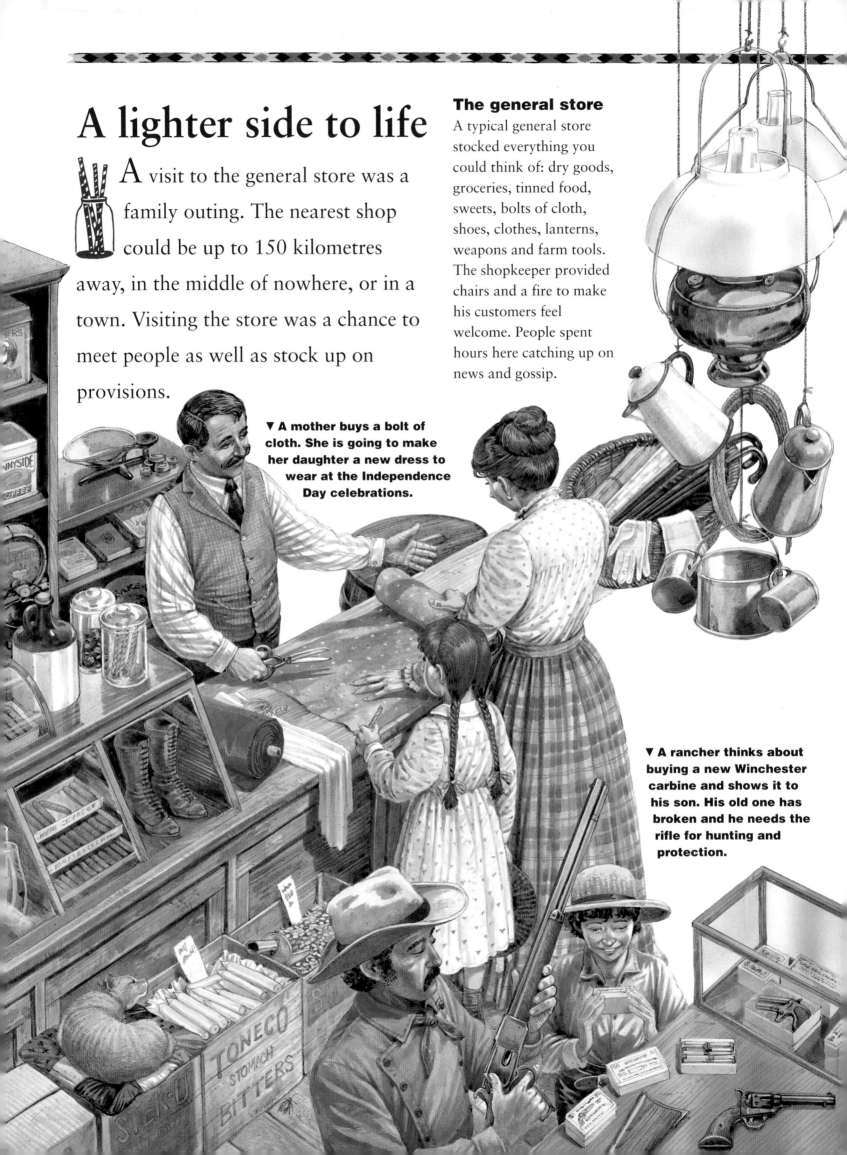

A lighter side to life

A visit to the general store was a family outing. The nearest shop could be up to 150 kilometres away, in the middle of nowhere, or in a town. Visiting the store was a chance to meet people as well as stock up on provisions.

The general store

A typical general store stocked everything you could think of: dry goods, groceries, tinned food, sweets, bolts of cloth, shoes, clothes, lanterns, weapons and farm tools. The shopkeeper provided chairs and a fire to make his customers feel welcome. People spent hours here catching up on news and gossip.

▼ A mother buys a bolt of cloth. She is going to make her daughter a new dress to wear at the Independence Day celebrations.

▼ A rancher thinks about buying a new Winchester carbine and shows it to his son. His old one has broken and he needs the rifle for hunting and protection.

The wish book

Mail-order catalogues stocked everything from everyday items to luxuries. There was even a catalogue for the lonesome man who wished to order a bride!

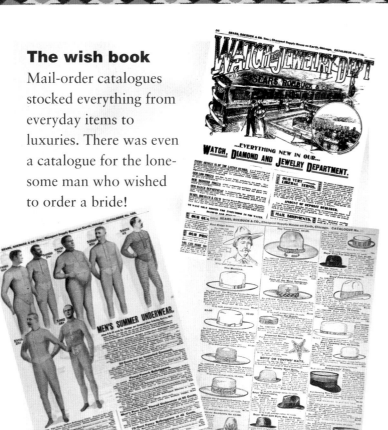

The quilting bee

Neighbouring homesteads were far apart. Women took a break from their chores and gathered at one another's homes to swap gossip and make quilts. These 'bees' lasted days – it could be ages before they got together again.

W hat little spare time settlers had, they liked to spend enjoying themselves. Every town in America held a parade to celebrate Independence Day. A wedding, a new house, or a barn-raising was a big event. So were dances, horse races, boxing matches and county fairs. There was plenty of food and drink, and a chance for people to meet old friends and make new ones.

Fun at the fair

There were many ways that teenage boys could show off their strength and skills at the county fair. Pig-wrestling was dirty and fun. Other contests were frog-jumping, foot races, games of catch and even baseball.

Mine
In search of the rich veins of gold, miners used pickaxes and dynamite to dig cave-like mines in the mountain-side. The rubble was then shovelled into the sluice.

Sluice
As the rubble from the mine passed down the long sluice, or trough, water washed away the lighter debris to leave behind the heavier gold buried inside the rock.

Cash office
Inside the cash or assays office, gold dust and nuggets were weighed and traded for ready cash.

Laundry
Many Chinese were discriminated against in the gold mines. They found a way to make money out of the Gold Rush by opening camp laundries.

Gold Rush!

"Gold! Gold on the American River!" With these words, Sam Brannan started the 1849 rush of fortune-seekers to California. Some came overland along the Oregon Trail; others sailed to San Francisco. Known as the forty-niners, the prospectors included more than 17,000 Chinese immigrants. Mining camps, or diggings, sprang up with names like Sixbit Gulch, Whiskey Flat and Hangtown.

Fortunes
A miner working his own diggings could make lots of money. Twenty-five grams of gold was worth $16. Working seven days a week, a miner could find enough gold to earn himself almost $2,000.

California wasn't the only place with gold. The Black Hills of Dakota were sacred lands for the northern Plains tribes, and lands that the government had promised them they could keep. But after the 7th Cavalry found gold in the region, thousands of gold-seekers headed for the hills.

Community

At the diggings, miners of the same nationality soon found themselves living close together. They were very protective of their mines and looked after one another.

Muleback tuck shop

Miners didn't have time to waste cooking luxuries like bread. So they were willing to part with a dollar a loaf when the baker came by with freshly-baked bread. Women soon found they could make money by charging for meals. Some went on to be successful hotel owners.

▲ As fast as they sprang up, the mining towns also disappeared. Once every last bit of gold had been mined, there was nothing to keep people there. They packed their bags and headed for the next diggings, leaving a 'ghost town' behind them.

Panning for gold

There were several ways to get gold out of the creek. One man would put rubble from the river-bed into a 'rocker' as another man moved it back and forth in the flow of water – any gold was caught in a sieve below. Panning was another cheap and easy method. A handful of gravel or sand was put into a pan, then swirled around with water to wash away the lighter sand, leaving the heavy gold behind.

THE MAIN SITES OF TOMBSTONE

1 St Paul's Episcopal Church (under construction)
2 Mexican quarter
3 Hop Town – the Chinese quarter
4 new Cochise County Courthouse (under construction)
5 C.S. Fly's photographic studio
6 newspaper office: *Tombstone Epitaph*
7 City Hall (under construction)
8 original Courthouse
9 newspaper office: *Tombstone Nugget*
10 Schieffelin Hall (theatre)
11 post office
12 Jack Crabtree's Lexington livery stable
13 Catholic church (under construction)
14 women's boarding houses
15 Wells Fargo office
16 ice-cream parlour
17 OK Corral
18 US customs office
19 Occidental Saloon
20 Watt & Tarbell's undertaking parlour
21 The Crystal Palace Saloon (US Deputy Marshal's office above)
22 The Oriental Saloon
23 city bakery
24 The Birdcage Theater
25 Western Union telegraph office
26 courtroom
27 first public school (temporary)
28 Wing Woo Lung laundry
29 miners' cabins
30 fire station

Why 'Tombstone'?

When Ed Schieffelin's party began prospecting in Arizona, someone said all they were likely to find would be tombstones. Instead they struck silver, but they named the new settlement 'Tombstone'!

A frontier town

Not all towns in the West depended on the cattle trade for their existence. The discovery of rich mineral deposits could herald the coming of a frontier town. Tombstone, Arizona began this way when silver was discovered there by prospector Ed Schieffelin in 1877.

SIXTH STREET

30

Town folk

There were many people in town who depended on the success of Tombstone's mines for their livelihood. The miners came from different cultures and businesses sprang up to cater for everyone's needs. There were newspapers, saloons, hotels, schools and churches.

JOBS IN TOMBSTONE
1 newspaper editor
2 undertaker
3 blacksmith
4 travelling preacher
5 actress
6 school teacher
7 mayor

Allen Street

Allen Street was one of Tombstone's main roads. It was lined with shops, hotels, banks and saloons.

The street was nearly 25 metres wide. It had raised wooden sidewalks instead of paving stones, and no street lights.

Tombstone is the site of the most famous gunfight in the West. Yet the gunfight at the OK Corral lasted only 30 seconds. Wyatt Earp, his brothers Morgan and Virgil, and Doc Holliday fought Ike and Billy Clanton, and Tom and Frank McLaury to end a long feud. The McLaurys and Billy Clanton were killed; Morgan and Virgil Earp and Doc Holliday were wounded.

A hard life

Many men became soldiers to escape poverty, the law, or to start a new life. Army life was hard and many deserted. Poor supplies meant most food was maggot-infested. The soldiers lacked equipment and clothing. Only the officers lived in comfort. There was even a billiards room for them. The only entertainment for the ordinary soldiers was drinking in the bar.

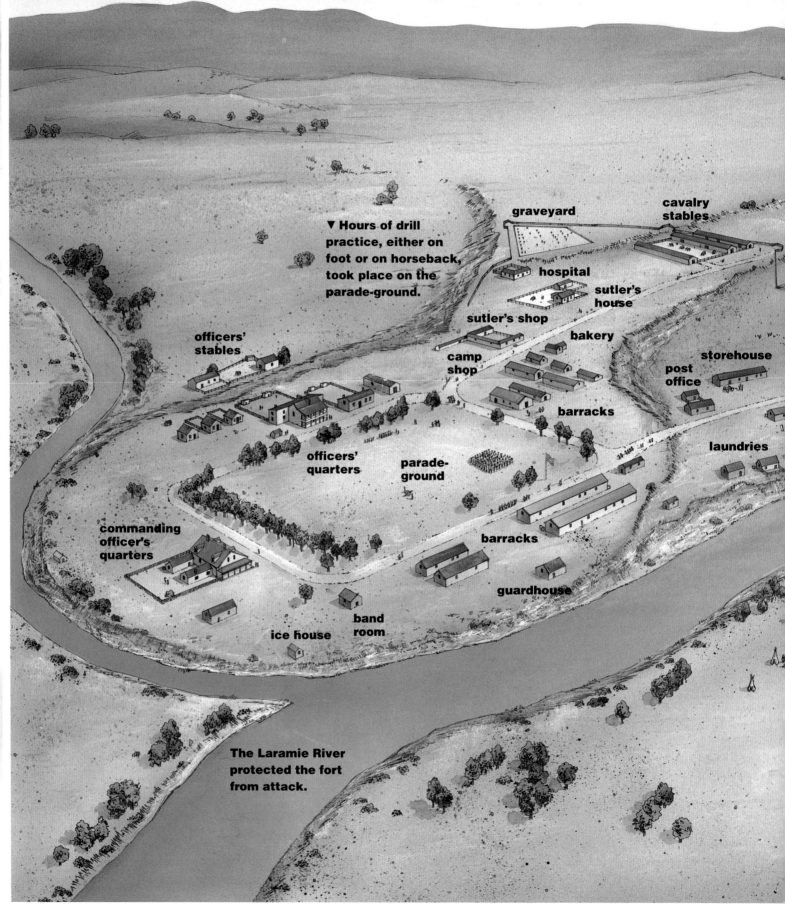

▼ Hours of drill practice, either on foot or on horseback, took place on the parade-ground.

graveyard

cavalry stables

hospital

sutler's house

sutler's shop

bakery

officers' stables

camp shop

storehouse

post office

barracks

officers' quarters

parade-ground

laundries

commanding officer's quarters

barracks

guardhouse

ice house

band room

The Laramie River protected the fort from attack.

FORT LIFE

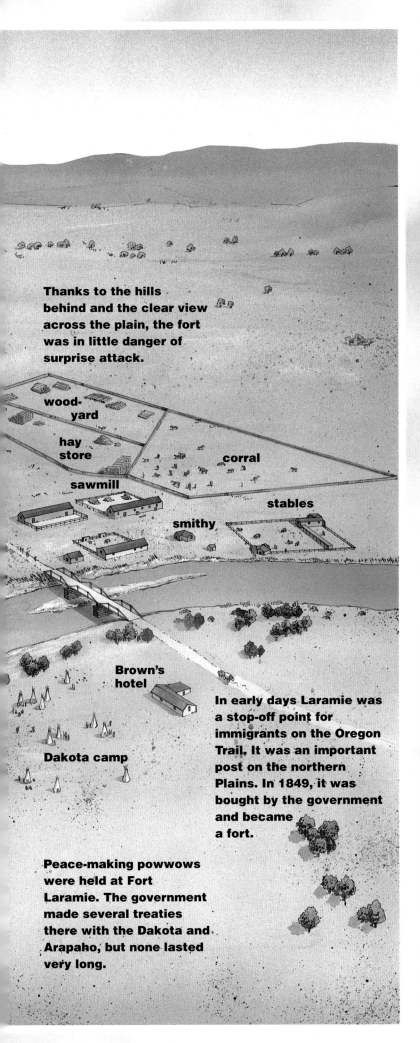

As the West was settled, the army was called in to protect the pioneers against American Indians who were resisting being driven from their homelands. Forts made important bases where the army could house its peace-keeping troops. They were well-defended and rarely attacked. As the frontier grew, more and more forts were built, especially during the Indian Wars. Many smaller defences – called posts, garrisons, or camps – were also built, at strategic sites along the trails, such as river crossings or junctions.

Thanks to the hills behind and the clear view across the plain, the fort was in little danger of surprise attack.

wood-yard

hay store

sawmill

corral

smithy

stables

Brown's hotel

Dakota camp

In early days Laramie was a stop-off point for immigrants on the Oregon Trail. It was an important post on the northern Plains. In 1849, it was bought by the government and became a fort.

Peace-making powwows were held at Fort Laramie. The government made several treaties there with the Dakota and Arapaho, but none lasted very long.

Fort Davis, Texas
This campaign fort once housed soldiers of the 9th and 10th Cavalry and the 24th and 25th Infantry. It was abandoned in 1891. Today it is a national monument.

Men at arms

The protection of the United States in the early days was entrusted to a small army of professional soldiers and volunteer citizens. These men were not well trained or armed. Many were immigrants who were unable to speak English.

The army was responsible for surveying the land, and defending the pioneers and the crews building the railroad. Even during the Civil War, when men left to fight for the North or South, the army still looked after the frontier.

Corporal, US Dragoons (1840s)
Mounted soldiers, such as the 1st Dragoons, protected the wagon trains from American Indian attacks as they trundled along the Santa Fe Trail. They were issued with a rifle (a single shot M1836 Hall carbine .64 calibre), and a wickedly sharp sabre.

Buffalo soldiers
This painting by Frederic Remington is called *Buffalo Soldiers*. This was the nickname given to black soldiers by American Indians, as their hair reminded them of buffalo hair: short and curly. There were four all-black units – two cavalry and two infantry.

Private, Union Infantry (1861–1865)
In the Civil War, the soldiers of the Union were fighting for a united America. Their blue uniform was standard issue based on the early military design that got them the nickname of 'blue bellies'. When the Civil War came to an end, many soldiers were posted to forts and garrisons in the West to keep the frontier open and to fight in the Indian Wars.

Private, Infantry (1890s)

The soldier's uniform and weapons changed little over the years. The Springfield rifle was adapted from the Civil War muzzle-loader so it could take the same ammunition as the soldier's pistol. By the end of 1890 the soldier's job in the West was done. The American Indians were defeated and the West settled.

The army was responsible for building roads and exploring new routes into the West. The Transport Corps carried supplies and once even experimented with camels to carry loads in the desert! When Yellowstone National Park was established in 1872, the army was drafted in to look after that, too.

Call to arms!

The Civil War between the Union North and Confederate South began in 1861 when Confederates attacked Union troops at Fort Sumter. Every able-bodied man was called to fight for his beliefs.

Junior officer, Confederate Cavalry (1861–1865)

Often known as 'Johnny Reb', the Confederate soldier fought for southern independence in the Civil War. The Confederates believed that they should be allowed to keep black slaves and that southern states should be free of northern government. Their 'Rebel Yell' was a blood-curdling battle-cry that frightened many soldiers of the Union.

Cap badges

Each regiment had its own distinctive badge. Worn on the cap, their designs have hardly changed to this day.

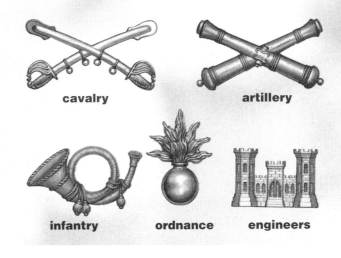

cavalry   artillery

infantry   ordnance   engineers

Into battle

The army was famous for its campaigns against the American Indians. Between 1865 and 1890 the conflict between the two sides brought many deaths. The army had more advanced weapons but the American Indian tribes knew the lie of the land and were more mobile. The Battle of the Little Big Horn in 1876 was the most spectacular victory for the American Indians over the US army. It also proved to be their last.

'General' Custer

George Armstrong Custer was a keen soldier. He wanted to be a general but only reached the permanent rank of lieutenant-colonel. He led the 7th Cavalry in many victorious campaigns against the Plains tribes until his death at the Battle of the Little Big Horn.

Sitting Bull

Tatonka-I-Yaktanka (Sitting Buffalo Bull) was the medicine man of the Hunkpapa tribe of the Teton Dakota. He was also a politician who influenced the Cheyenne and Arapaho. He united the Dakota sub-tribes and became a respected and feared war chief.

Battle of the Little Big Horn

On June 22, 1876, against orders, Custer led the 7th Cavalry in an attack on an Indian village at the Little Big Horn River, Montana. Led by great war chiefs such as Gall, Crazy Horse and Sitting Bull, the Cheyenne and Dakota warriors killed Custer and all his men.

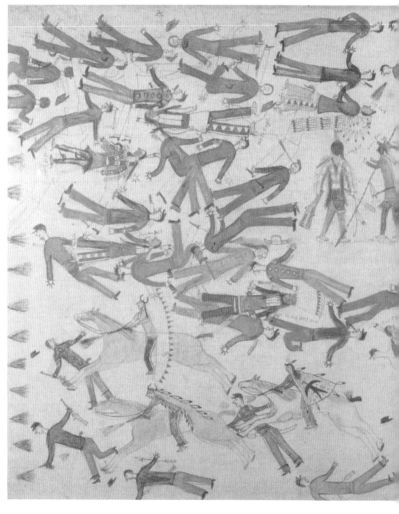

▲ *Custer's Last Stand*, by Edgar S. Paxson

In battles after 1876, the army made a determined effort to beat the tribes into submission. With the defeat of Chief Joseph of the Nez Percé in 1877, white victory seemed certain. By the late 1880s only the Apaches were still fighting, led by such leaders as Cochise and Geronimo.

'The Great Father sends us presents and wants us to sell him the road, but the White Chief comes with soldiers to steal it before the Indian says yes or no. I will talk with you no more. I will go now and I will fight you!'

RED CLOUD

Indian Wars

As the spread of immigrants grew, the government broke its promise to the American Indians that it only wanted enough tribal land for the wagon trains to cross. Indian land was claimed for homesteads, railroads and mines. Some tribes retaliated and attacked settlers, stage-coaches and miners. The army was called in and regional battles flared.

Massacre at Wounded Knee

On December 29, 1890, a unit of the 7th Cavalry rounded up over 300 Dakota Indians at Wounded Knee Creek, South Dakota. As the soldiers were disarming the men, a shot was fired and the soldiers fired back. Within minutes the army had slaughtered the Dakota and ended the American Indian opposition to the white Americans.

In this Dakota painting of the Battle of the Little Big Horn, Custer lies dead, wearing his famous yellow buckskins.

DEADLY DAYS

Outlaws were a threat to the frontier way of life. Some people stole rather than worked for a living. There were stage-coach robbers, cattle rustlers, land barons (who stole other people's claims), gamblers and train robbers – to name but a few.

Stage-coaches

Before the railroad was built, the stage was the main form of transport for passengers and mail. There were many types of stage-coach, but none more famous than the Wells Fargo *Concorde*.

The loot

Passenger stage-coaches often carried money. The strongbox held company payrolls in coins or gold, and this was the robbers' main target. Of course, they robbed the passengers as well!

The gang

Outlaws operated alone or in gangs. The Hole in the Wall Gang – if records are to be believed – had over one hundred members from different gangs, including the Wild Bunch led by Butch Cassidy.

The one thing that an outlaw's life depended on was his weapon. Early revolvers had paper cartridges with lead bullets and were classed as cap and ball pistols. These were later replaced with brass-jacketed bullets of different calibres (or sizes). The revolver was used for fighting at close quarters, the rifle or carbine for long-distance shooting. The threat of a shotgun was enough to scare anyone, and many outlaws sawed down the barrel to make the weapon easier to carry.

WEAPONS OF THE WEST
1 Loomis IXL no. 15 shotgun
2 Winchester M1866 carbine
   .44 calibre
3 Sharps M1863 carbine
   .52 calibre
4 Le Mat M1856
   .40 calibre
5 Walker Colt M1874
   revolver .44 calibre
6 Colt New Model Army
   'Peacemaker' M1873
   .45 calibre
7 Smith & Wesson
   Model Army
   'Russian' no. 3
   revolver
   .44 calibre

(1867–*c.* 1910)
Once a cavalry scout, the Apache Kid killed a man, escaped and went on to become a ruthless killer and robber who menaced New Mexico and Arizona.

(1848–1889)
Belle Starr was the leader of a gang of horse and cattle rustlers. She and her Cherokee husband, Sam, had a $1,000 reward on their heads.

(1853–1895)
Hardin was one of the most feared gunmen in Texas. After killing a black slave, he ambushed and killed the three Union soldiers sent to arrest him.

(1876–unknown)
Cattle Annie once rode with the Doolin Gang. She and her partner, Little Britches, were famous cattle rustlers, known as 'Oklahoma's girl bandits'.

Billy the Kid (1859–1881)
He was only 22 years old when he died, but William H. Bonney, or Billy the Kid, left his mark. He killed his first man when he was 12 years old and was involved in a ranch war known as the Lincoln County War. After 'the Kid' killed two deputies in New Mexico, Sheriff Pat Garrett hunted him down and shot him.

Outlaws and gunslingers

The best-known outlaws were the man-killers. Bloody Bill Anderson, Rufus Buck, Joaquin Murieta and John Brown were all cold-blooded murderers. After fighting in the Civil War, some, such as Frank and Jesse James, couldn't fit back into normal civilian life. They took to robbery with a large gang of other ex-soldiers. Lone bandit Black Bart eluded the law for eight years, robbing Wells Fargo stages. He had come to California to seek his fortune, and had tried his hand at panning for gold before taking up his life of crime.

James Butler Hickok, or Wild Bill Hickok was made into a living legend by newpapers and magazines. He was an army scout, Indian fighter, pony express employee and lawman in several towns. He wore twin Colt Navy .36s in cross-draw fashion and was a deadly shot.

Fast on the draw

'Fanning' a revolver is the fastest way to fire more than one bullet. Gripping the butt of the pistol in one hand, with the index finger holding back the trigger (1), the palm of the other hand hauls back (or fans) the hammer (2) once for each bullet to be fired. As the pistol comes up level, the hammer is fully cocked and springs forward in one go (3).

Gunslingers

To be called a gunslinger meant that you were on the right side of the law, as well as a good man with a gun. Other names for these men were 'gunsman', 'gunny' or 'gun shark'. Whether he wore one pistol or two, a gunslinger's weapons were always on display to show he meant business – he would always use his pistols first and ask questions later.

Law and order

Coping with criminals on the frontier was a problem. The vastness of the area was too much for the official police force. In some places ordinary men became vigilantes and fought the outlaws themselves. The Cattle Ranchers Association hired range detectives to catch rustlers. Gunslingers were hired to guard banks, railroads and mines. The most famous peace-officer was the marshal. Towns hired marshals and deputies to enforce their laws.

Law west of the Pecos

Roy Bean was nearly 60 years old when he came to the little town of Langtry, Texas and became Justice of the Peace. Self-taught in law, he set up a courtroom in his saloon where he was judge for almost 20 years. He was in love with the English actress Lily Langtry and named his saloon the Jersey Lilly after her. Known for his strange rulings, he once fined a dead man $40 for illegally carrying a weapon!

Badge of office

Law officers wore badges to show what job they held. There were many designs, just as there were different jobs. A US marshal was responsible for the whole state. The town marshal and deputies looked after the town for the government. The protection of local people, homes and businesses was down to the sheriff and his deputies. The famed Texas Rangers were formed by Stephen F. Austin in 1823 to help enforce the law and they still operate today.

Pinkerton

Civil War veteran Allen Pinkerton's Detective Agency made a business out of capturing wanted men. The agency fought against the James Gang and the Wild Bunch. It was the first to keep files, with details of solved and unsolved crimes and photographs of criminals, like the files used by the FBI today.

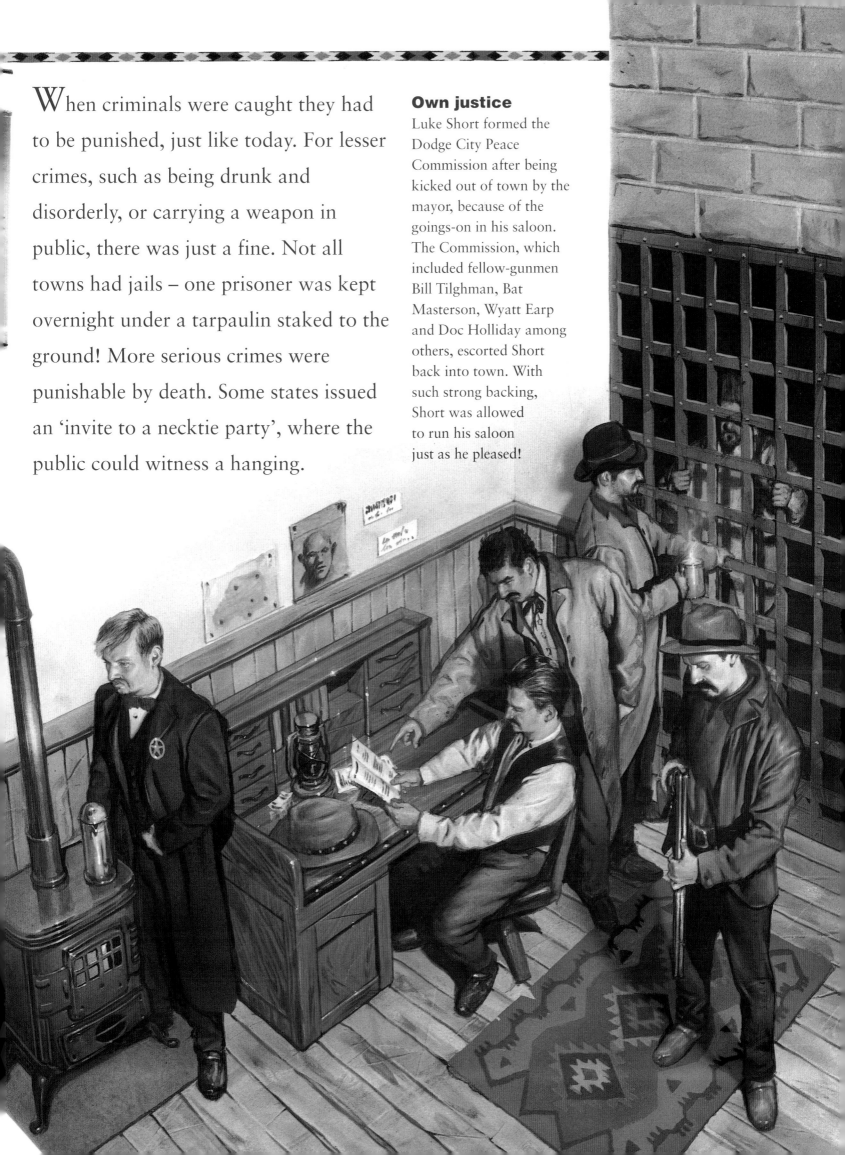

When criminals were caught they had to be punished, just like today. For lesser crimes, such as being drunk and disorderly, or carrying a weapon in public, there was just a fine. Not all towns had jails – one prisoner was kept overnight under a tarpaulin staked to the ground! More serious crimes were punishable by death. Some states issued an 'invite to a necktie party', where the public could witness a hanging.

Own justice

Luke Short formed the Dodge City Peace Commission after being kicked out of town by the mayor, because of the goings-on in his saloon. The Commission, which included fellow-gunmen Bill Tilghman, Bat Masterson, Wyatt Earp and Doc Holliday among others, escorted Short back into town. With such strong backing, Short was allowed to run his saloon just as he pleased!

STEEL TRACKS

Railroads were built to provide a speedy transport system that spanned the continent. They often ran right through American Indian land, despite previous government promises. Troops had to guard the railroaders. Work started on the transcontinental railroad in 1863. Ex-soldiers and Irishmen headed west from Omaha, building the Union Pacific line. Chinese railroaders headed east from San Francisco, with the Central Pacific. On May 10, 1869 the two lines met at Promontory Point, Utah.

Railroad routes

Railroads were a fast way of transporting goods, mail and people across deserts, prairies and mountains. Cattle drives ended where their trail met the tracks at a cow town. The map shows the railroad lines built in the 1860s and some of the towns that they connected.

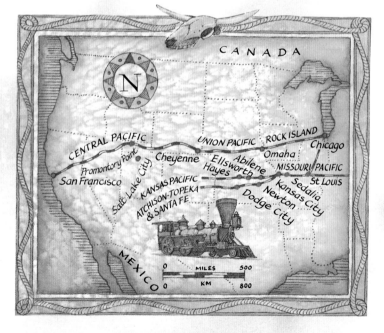

Explosion

Where tracks had to be laid through a mountain, specialist workers called 'graders' blasted tunnels with dynamite. It was a dangerous job and the powerful explosives led to many accidents. Pickaxes and shovels were used, too, and mule-drawn carts took away the rocks and rubble.

Communication

Telegraph lines often already lined the railroad's route. Telegraph messages could be sent in seconds to company headquarters.

Tent town

The railroad workers lived in makeshift towns, known as 'hell on wheels'. Most of the men slept in tents, which were easy to pitch and pack up.

Building bridges

Obstacles such as valleys and rivers were no match for the engineers. They built trestle-bridges of iron and wood and suspension bridges spanning over 300 metres in length.

Supplies

Everything from food, water, rolling-stock, machinery and the rails themselves had to be taken to the site either by track already laid or by horse-drawn wagons.

As hard as they tried, the American Indians couldn't stop the 'iron road'.

The iron horse

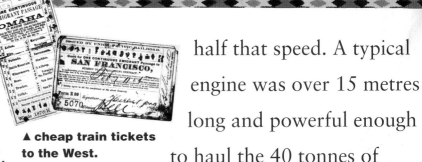

▲ cheap train tickets to the West.

The American Indians called the train the 'iron horse'. It was the classic American steam locomotive (with a 4-4-0 engine) that became the workhorse of the railroad. Passenger trains reached nearly 30 kph, although heavily-laden goods trains managed only half that speed. A typical engine was over 15 metres long and powerful enough to haul the 40 tonnes of train along. Behind the engine, the tender carried wood for the fire and over 9,000 litres of water for the boiler that produced the steam to power the engine.

Pullman coach

tender

Tickets and times

The fare from Kansas City to Denver cost $65 (six weeks' wages for a cowboy). Timetables showed the different routes and local times. In 1863, the Railway Association divided the United States into the four time zones which are still in use today.

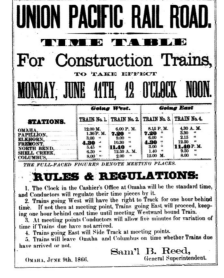

UNION PACIFIC RAIL ROAD.
TIME TABLE
For Construction Trains,
TO TAKE EFFECT
MONDAY, JUNE 11TH, 12 O'CLOCK NOON.

	Going West.		Going East	
STATIONS.	TRAIN No 1.	TRAIN No 2.	TRAIN No 3.	TRAIN No 4.
OMAHA,	12.00 M.	6.00 P. M.	8.15 P. M.	4.30 A. M.
PAPILLION,	1.30 P. M.	7.30	7.30	3.30
ELKHORN,	3.00	9.00	6.00	2.15
FREMONT,	4.30	10.30	4.30	12.50
NORTH BEND,	5.45	11.40	3.00	11.40 P.M.
SHELL CREEK,	6.50	12.50 A. M.	1.40	9.50
COLUMBUS,	8.00	2.00	12.00 M.	8.00

THE FULL-FACED FIGURES DENOTE MEETING PLACES.

RULES & REGULATIONS:

1. The Clock in the Cashier's Office at Omaha will be the standard time, and Conductors will regulate their time pieces by it.
2. Trains going West will have the right to Track for one hour behind time. If not then at meeting point, Trains going East will proceed, keeping one hour behind card time until meeting Westward bound Train.
3. At meeting points Conductors will allow five minutes for variation of time if Trains due have not arrived.
4. Trains going East will Side Track at meeting points.
5. Trains will leave Omaha and Columbus on time whether Trains due have arrived or not.

Sam'l B. Reed,
General Superintendent.
OMAHA, JUNE 9th, 1866.

Trains replaced stages as the main way of carrying payrolls across the country. And, like stage-coaches, they got robbed. The first American train robbery took place in 1866, when the Reno Gang held up the Ohio and Mississippi Railroad and got away with $10,000.

▼ The driver sounded a large steam whistle to warn of the train's approach.

spark-arrester

whistle

safety valve

funnel

bell

steam dome

head-light

boiler

cylinder

driving wheels

bogie wheels

cowcatcher

All aboard!

There was stiff competition between the railroad companies. To attract customers, companies advertised on colourful posters. They promised the fastest journey, most comfortable berths, or even that their crews were supplied with ammunition in case of attack!

In the driving seat

The driver and his mate stayed in the cab feeding the hungry fire in the engine with large wooden logs. The cab was built of varnished walnutwood and the engineer's seat of ash.

Cowcatcher

A large metal triangle was fitted at the front of the train. The 'cowcatcher' not only pushed stray cattle off the tracks, it also cleared any snowdrifts or loose rocks out of the way.

Spark-arrester

A wire mesh over the funnel stopped any stray sparks escaping and setting the dry plains alight.

The 'end' of the West

In 1890, the Bureau of the Census claimed that "no frontiers remained" in the United States. The days of the Wild West were over. No single factor decided it – the railroad now bridged East and West, the prairies and plains were settled, the American Indians had been forced onto reservations. Yet the West was still growing. New rail routes were being built, Arizona and Utah were yet to join the Union, and immigrants still arrived in San Francisco in their thousands. This time the lure was not gold or land, but oil.

KEY

1 Makah 1855	44 Pueblo Indians 1858	83 Cherokee 1828
2 Ozette 1893	45 Zuni 1877	84 Peoria 1867
3 Quileute 1889	46 Mescalero Apache 1873	84 Modoc 1874
4 Hoh River 1893	47 Hopi 1882	84 Ottawa 1867
5 Quinalelt 1855	48 Havasupai 1880	84 Shawnee 1831
6 Shoalwater 1865	49 Salt River 1879	84 Seneca 1831
7 Chehalis 1864	50 Northern Cheyenne 1884	84 Wyandot 1867
8 Umatilla 1855	51 Colville 1872	85 Creek 1833
9 Grande Ronde 1857	52 Spokane 1881	86 Choctaw 1820
10 Warm Springs 1853	53 Coeur d'Alene 1867	87 Seminole 1833
11 Klamath 1864	54 Jocko 1855	88 Chickasaw 1837
12 Hoopa Valley 1864	55 Blackfeet 1875	89 Kiowa & Comanche 1865
13 Round Valley 1856	56 Fort Belknap 1888	90 Winnebago 1865
14 Pyramid Lake 1874	57 Fort Peck 1868	91 Omaha 1854
15 Walker River 1874	58 Crow 1868	92 Red Lake 1863
16 Tule River 1873	59 Crow Creek 1889	93 White Earth 1867
17 Moapa River 1873	60 Lower Brule 1889	94 Vermilion Lake 1881
18 Hualpai 1863	61 Devil's Lake 1867	95 Mille Lac 1855
19 Colorado River 1863	62 Turtle Mountain 1882	96 La Pointe 1854
20 Mission Indians 1875	63 Fort Berthold 1870	97 Lac Courte Oreille 1854
21 Gila Bend 1882	64 Standing Rock 1868	98 Ontonagon 1854
22 Yuma 1884	65 Cheyenne River 1889	99 L'Anse 1854
23 Gila River 1859	66 Pine Ridge 1889	100 Lac du Flambeau 1854
24 Papago 1874	67 Sioux 1882	101 Menominee 1854
25 White Mountain 1871	68 Rosebud 1889	102 Stockbridge 1856
26 Lummi 1855	69 Ponca 1881	103 Isbella 1855
27 Swinomish 1855	70 Otoe & Missouri 1881	104 Tuscarora 1797
28 Tulalip 1855	71 Pawnee 1876	105 Tonawanda 1797
29 Puyallup 1854	72 Sac & Fox 1867	106 Cattaraugus 1797
30 Muckleshoot 1857	73 Iowa 1883	107 Oil Spring 1797
31 Squaxon Island 1854	74 Pottawatomie 1867	108 Allegany 1797
32 Skokomish 1855	75 Wichita 1872	109 Onondaga 1788
33 Port Madison 1855	76 Arapaho & Cheyenne 1869	110 Oneida 1788
34 Yakima 1855	77 Sac and Fox 1867	111 St. Regis 1796
35 Lapwal 1863	78 Sac and Fox 1836	112 Eastern Cherokee 1874
36 Lemhl 1875	79 Kickapoo 1832	113 Seminole 1894
37 Uintah Valley 1861	80 Pottawatomie 1837	
38 Wind River 1861	81 Kansas 1872	
39 Fort Hall 1868	82 Osage 1870	
40 Duck Valley 1877		
41 Navajo 1868		
42 Ute 1863		
43 Jicarilla Apache 1874		

▲ The map shows American Indian reservations at the end of the century and the dates they were established. As their homelands were taken away, tribes were forced onto these reservations. Their traditional way of life was destroyed and they could no longer support themselves.

Changing prairies

The settlers changed the face of the West. They brought water to the dry prairies, using windmills to pump water from below ground. Desolate, arid land was cultivated and became rich farm land.

Death of the range

The open-range style of raising cattle became a thing of the past as barbed-wire fenced in the land. Many ranchers turned to sheep-farming – sheep were cheaper to keep and could be sold at higher profits.

Land rush

The last piece of land to be taken away from the American Indians was Oklahoma, known at the time as the Indian Territory. This was in 1889 and sparked off the last mad scramble for land.

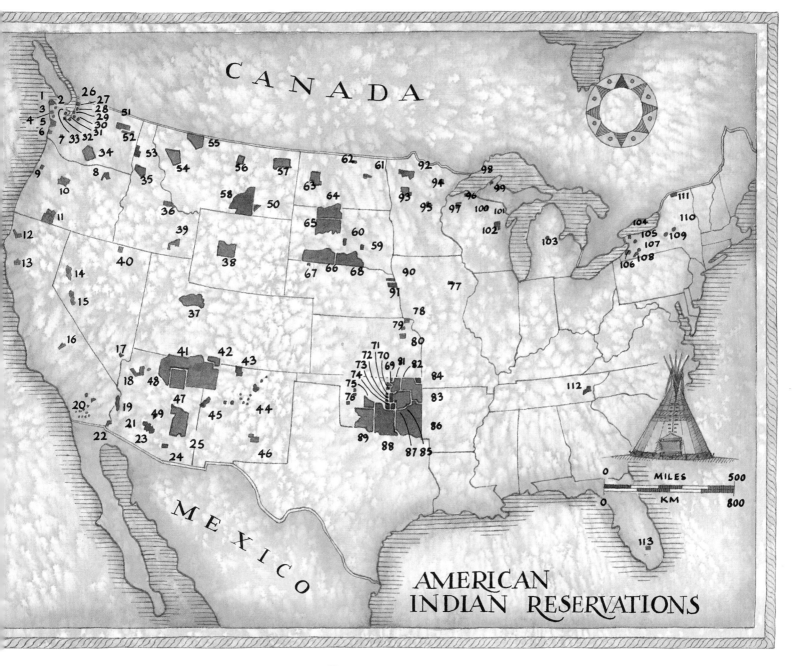

C A N A D A

M E X I C O

AMERICAN
INDIAN RESERVATIONS

0 MILES 500

0 KM 800

Goodbye buffalo?

From 1872 to 1876, a
staggering four million
buffalo were killed. To
preserve the dwindling
herds, the government
forbade hunting buffalo
in Yellowstone Park,
Wyoming, the country's
first conservation area.

The outlaws

Lawlessness didn't end
with the Wild West. Such
infamous outlaws as Butch
Cassidy and the Sundance
Kid continued to operate
into the 20th century.

Gushing oil wells in Texas and
California promised fortunes to be
made. The first find was at Corsicana,
Texas in 1894. Drilling for water,
workers struck oil instead. Just as the
forty-niners had invaded California,
fortune-seekers poured into Texas. Oil
'fever' spread throughout the West and
boomtowns sprang up. The West still
promised wealth and a new life.

The entertaining West

1

Even as the Wild West was coming to an end, the legend was being born – there were rodeo events, books and magazines, and the first Wild West shows, such as Buffalo Bill's. All created an exciting image of the days of the frontier. Cinema and TV rediscovered the Wild West and presented daring – though not especially truthful – tales of heroes and villains.

2

3

Read all about it!

The West is a rich source of exciting stories. Authors have used the West as a setting for romance (1), or to rewrite history with exaggerated tales of cowboys and Indians (2). Popular TV series created their own spin-offs for readers (3). Even at the time, cheap magazines and dime novels churned out short stories by the thousand. The 'soap operas' of their day, these publications didn't paint an accurate picture of the West, but readers avidly followed the adventures of Pawnee Bill (4), Arizona Joe and other heroes.

All the thrill of the show

Buffalo Bill Cody travelled the world with his Wild West Show in the 1880s. Whooping Indians, dashing cowboys and mock stage-coach robberies thrilled huge audiences. Annie Oakley was one of the stars of the show. She was nicknamed 'Little Miss Sure-Shot' by the Dakota chief Sitting Bull, who also toured with the show.

4

Rodeo riders

The rodeo is a dazzling contest of riding and roping skills. It started as an informal chance to show off. Today there are nearly 3,000 rodeo events in the world each year.

▶ **Prairie Rose Henderson, 1900s: was she the first female bronc-buster?**

The West hits the small screen

Television series about the West peaked in the 1960s. *Bonanza* (above) was one of the most popular and ran for 14 years. Other TV shows included *Wagon Train*, *The Lone Ranger*, *Gunsmoke*, *High Chaparral* and *Little House on the Prairie*.

The first cowboy films or 'Westerns' appeared in 1903. Film-makers mostly chose to ignore the real West in favour of hold-ups and gunfights. These were far more exciting than the homesteaders' grinding toil! Frontier life was misrepresented in other ways, too. According to Hollywood, there were no black or American Indian cowboys. The lead in *Tomahawk* (1952), a film about black mountain man Jim Beckwourth, was played by a white actor.

◄ **Bill Pickett: in 1881 he became the first cowboy to bulldog (wrestle) a steer.**

▼ **Not all Westerns are about cowboys. *How the West Was Won* (1962) tells the story of a pioneer family's struggle to settle the new land.**

Screen heroes

For many, the cowboy is summed up by the heroic parts played by John Wayne (above), Clint Eastwood or Kevin Costner. Early Hollywood films wanted lone heroes; they didn't show how a cowboy – or outlaw – often depended on others for his life. Colourful individuals soon stood out: but where would Wyatt Earp be without his brothers, or Jesse James without his gang?

Characters of the West

Thomas Hart Benton (1782–1858)

As a politician representing Mississippi, championed the cause for America's 'Manifest Destiny' – the right of the US to expand its land westward.

John Butterfield (1801–1869)

Operated the Butterfield Overland Mail Service between Missouri and San Francisco from 1858 to 1861. He sold the firm to Wells Fargo and went on to develop a new venture – American Express.

Martha Jane Canary (Calamity Jane) (c. 1848–1903)

Many stories abound about Jane but she definitely loved Wild Bill Hickok and is buried next to him in Deadwood, Dakota. She was a good shot, often dressed as a man and drove wagon teams for the Union Pacific Railroad.

Christopher (Kit) Carson (1809–1868)

Famed as a fur trapper, explorer, scout and Indian fighter. Carson spoke French, Spanish and Indian languages.

Cochise (c. 1815–1874)

Renegade chief of the Chiricahua Apaches. He led his warriors on raids on settlers and miners throughout Arizona and even into Mexico.

William F. Cody (Buffalo Bill) (1846–1917)

The dime novelist Ned Buntline wrote of Buffalo Bill's exploits in 1869. Cody rode the pony express and was an army scout. In 1883 he began his famous Wild West Show.

Samuel Colt (1814–1862)

Designed a new, more reliable six-shooter by adapting the old five-shot revolver. His .45 'Peacemaker' was one of the most widely-used guns in the West.

Crazy Horse (Tashunka Witco) (c. 1841–1877)

One of the most aggressive Dakota chiefs who fought at Rosebud and Little Big Horn.

George Crook (1828–1890)

Army general who campaigned against the Apache and Dakota. He tried to get better treatment for Geronimo and other Apaches after their surrender.

Isom Dart (c. 1849–1900)

Born a slave, he fought with the Confederates. He became a cattle rustler and bronc-buster. He ended his days a rancher.

John Deere (1804–1886)

Inventor of the self-polishing steel plough, used by the settlers on the plains. In 1836, he founded Deere & Co, a farm machinery company that still operates today.

Wyatt Berry Stapp Earp (1848–1929)

Lawman in Wichita, Dodge City and Tombstone. He owned gambling halls and saloons from the 1870s, but is best known for his involvement in the gunfight at the OK Corral.

Alice Fletcher (1838–1923)

A white woman who lived among American Indian tribes in Nebraska. In 1883, she became an Indian agent and helped survey the land to be shared among the tribes. The American Indians called her 'Measuring Woman'.

Captain John Charles Frémont (1818–1890)

Early explorer of the West, nicknamed 'Great Pathfinder'. Kit Carson was his guide. His wife's account of his journeys was a bestseller.

Pat F. Garrett (1850–1908)

Former buffalo hunter and cowboy, he was sheriff of Lincoln County when he killed Billy the Kid. He later became a rancher and was shot dead in a feud.

Geronimo (Goyathly) (1829–1909)

Chiricahua Apache who led his people against both Mexicans and Americans. He finally surrendered and lived on a Florida reservation from 1887.

Charles Goodnight
(1836–1929)
One of the great cattle barons. After success with Oliver Loving, he teamed up with fellow rancher John Adair in 1877. By 1888 he was worth $500,000.

Sam Houston (1793–1863)
He led the Texans at San Jacinto in the military drive to gain Texan independence from Mexico. In 1836 he was sworn in as the first president of the Republic of Texas.

Chief Joseph
(1832–1904)
Not wanting to fight over land, Chief Joseph moved his tribe, the Nez Percés. The army pursued them, starting a three-month battle. The chief surrendered and he and his tribe were put on a reservation.

Oliver Loving (1813–1867)
Trailed herds to Colorado and Illinois before the Civil War. In 1866, he teamed up with Charles Goodnight to combine herds and cowboys.

Susan Shelby Magoffin
(1827–1855)
The first white woman to travel the Santa Fe Trail. She wrote a diary which was published in 1926.

James W. Marshall
(1810–1885)
Carpenter working on the American River, whose discovery of gold led to the California Gold Rush of 1849.

William Barclay (Bat) Masterson (1853–1921)
Railroader, buffalo hunter, saloon owner and gambler who found fame as a lawman. He was elected sheriff of Ford County in 1877 and was later a Dodge City marshal.

Marie Gilbert (Lola) Montez (1818–1861)
Originally from Ireland, Lola was an actress of dazzling beauty who entertained the miners across the California gold region.

Annie Oakley (1860–1926)
Found fame in Buffalo Bill's Wild West Show as 'Little Miss Sure-Shot'. She could outshoot her husband, Frank Butler, a well-known exhibition shooter.

Isaac Parker (1838–1896)
An Arizona judge, whose handling of outlaws soon got him the nickname of the 'Hanging Judge'. He even built a set of gallows that could hang more than one person at a time.

Red Cloud (1822–1909)
Dakota chief who successfully defended his land and closed many settlers' routes. He became leader of the Indians on reservations, and after the signing of the Fort Laramie Treaty he forced the US government to keep its terms.

Sacajawea (1778– *either* 1812 *or* 1884)
The Shoshoni wife of French-Canadian fur trapper Toussant Charbonneau who acted as a guide and interpreter for the Corps of Discovery.

William Tecumseh Sherman (1820–1891)
A Union general famed for his Civil War exploits. After the war, he took control of building forts across the West. He was in charge of the entire US army between 1869 and 1884, leading aggressive campaigns against the American Indians.

John B. Stetson (1830–1906)
Hatmaker from Philadelphia whose famous hat, the Stetson, is sometimes also called Boss of the Plains, a John B or a JB.

William Matthew Tilghman (1854–1924)
Renowned as a buffalo hunter and crack shot, he served as Dodge City's first marshal. He moved to Oklahoma, where he was one of the 'Three Guardsmen' (along with Chris Madsen and Heck Thomas), who hunted down the Doolin and Dalton Gangs.

Sarah Winnemucca
(1844–1891)
Paiute who negotiated for better conditions for her tribe. In 1883 she wrote an autobiography, *Life Among the Paiutes*, telling the plight of her tribe.

Brigham Young (1801–1877)
Religious leader who led the Mormons from Nauvoo, Illinois, where they were being persecuted for their beliefs, to Utah to settle on the shores of the Great Salt Lake.

Glossary

assays office Where miners had their gold weighed and priced.

barracks Soldiers' sleeping quarters.

brand The mark burned into the hide of a cow or horse to show who owned it.

BRAND

bronc-buster Someone who tamed wild, 'unbroken' horses for cowboys to ride.

bronco A wild horse, a mustang.

buffalo Shaggy wild cattle, also known as American bison.

buffalo chip Dried buffalo dung used as fuel on the plains.

calibre The diameter of a bullet, measured in hundredths of an inch.

cap and ball Early revolver loaded at the front of the cylinder.

carbine A short, light rifle.

cartridge A small case holding a gun's gunpowder or bullets.

cattle baron Owner of a vast cattle empire. Also known as a cattle king.

cattle drive Herding a group of cattle along a trail to be sold.

chaps Tough leggings worn over a cowboy's trousers to protect the legs.

chuck wagon A mobile cook-house used on round-ups and cattle drives. The chuck box at the back stored food, utensils and medicine.

Civil War War between the northern and southern states of the US, 1861–1865.

claim To have the legal right over the ownership of a mine, farm or grazing land.

Conestoga wagon A boat-shaped load-carrying wagon used by the pioneers. It was usually pulled along by oxen.

conquistador A Spanish soldier who came to America in the 1500s in search of gold.

corral Fenced enclosure for cattle or horses.

coup stick A long, lance-like stick with a curved end used by American Indian warriors to touch their enemy but not kill.

cow town A town which sprang up on a cattle trail. Also known as a trail town or cattle town.

cross-draw Style of drawing a revolver where the holster is worn on the hip with the butt of the revolver facing forward. The hand crosses in front of the body to draw the revolver.

dogie (1) An orphan calf. (2) Nickname for cattle.

fanning A method of shooting a revolver quickly by pulling back the hammer and pulling the trigger at the same time.

frontier The furthest edge of land which is settled, beyond which the country is wild.

fort A military base.

gallows A purpose-built structure to hang people.

Great Father Name for the president of the United States used by American Indians.

gunslinger Someone skilled with a gun.

holster A pouch to hold a revolver.

land baron A man who seized land, sometimes not very honestly.

lariat A rope used for catching animals. Known around the West Coast as a lasso.

line rider A cowboy who rode to the farthest limit (the line) of a ranch, to stop cows from straying.

loot Stolen goods.

LARIAT

lynch To punish someone without a proper trial, usually by hanging.

marshal A town's law-enforcer. Also called a policeman.

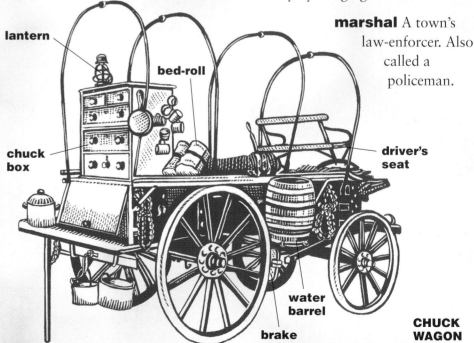

lantern

bed-roll

chuck box

driver's seat

water barrel

brake

CHUCK WAGON

maverick A calf without a brand.

Mormon A member of the Church of Jesus Christ of Latter-Day Saints, established in 1830.

panning Washing gravel in a pan so only the gold or silver is left behind.

PEACE PIPE

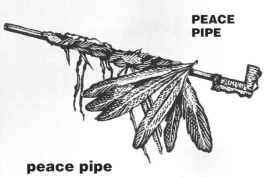

peace pipe A sacred American Indian object that invoked spiritual power when smoked. Also called a medicine pipe.

pemmican American Indian preserved food made of meat, berries and fat.

pony express A mail service between Missouri and California in 1860 and 1861. Riders covered the 3,164 kilometre trail in less than ten days.

powwow A ceremonial gathering of American Indians either for war, for peace talks, to socialise or dance.

prairie Open grassland.

ranch A cattle farm. It includes all the land, buildings and animals owned by the rancher.

remuda A herd of spare horses for cowboys.

Rendezvous The meeting between trappers and American Indians held every summer.

reservation Land put aside by the government for the use of one or more American Indian tribe.

revolver A handgun. Its chamber revolved to shoot six bullets. Also known as a six-shooter or pistol.

rocker A box or cradle used by gold miners. Gravel and water were rocked back and forth to sift out the dirt leaving the gold behind.

rodeo A contest of cowboy skills.

round-up The gathering together of cattle, for branding, by cowboys.

rustler A cattle or horse thief.

scalp A piece of scalp torn off as a sign of victory. Introduced by the Spanish, scalping was adopted by some American Indian tribes.

scout A guide or look-out.

settler Someone who makes a home in a place that is being populated for the first time. Also known as a pioneer.

skillet A metal frying pan.

slicker A waterproof coat.

soddy A dwelling made of sod turf built by settlers.

sougan A cowboy's closely-woven or quilted blanket.

stage-coach A horse-drawn coach for passengers and mail.

steer A male cow that is raised for beef.

Stetson A broad-brimmed, high-crowned felt hat, named after the hatmaker John B. Stetson.

stickball A ball game for two teams, on which lacrosse is based.

sutler A trader at an army post.

telegraph A way of sending Morse code messages electronically along a wire.

Texas tick A fever in Texas longhorn cattle that made them sick.

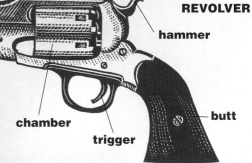

barrel · **REVOLVER** · hammer · chamber · trigger · butt

STETSON

tomahawk An American Indian war-axe.

totem American Indian name for an animal, such as an eagle, or inanimate thing, such as a river, considered to be a spiritual ancestor.

trapper Someone who made their living catching beaver and other wild animals for their fur.

tribe A community of American Indians who speak the same language and are bound together by ties of blood.

vaquero The name for a cowboy from the Southwest.

vigil A religious ceremony to mark an American Indian child's passage into adulthood.

vigilante Someone who takes the law into their own hands to gain justice.

war chief An American Indian leader in time of war, usually younger and less experienced than the chief of a tribe.

Wells Fargo Stage-coach company founded in 1852.

Winchester A rifle made by the Winchester Repeating Arms Co, known as 'the rifle that won the West'.

wish book A mail-order catalogue.

wrangler A man or boy who looked after the horses on a ranch or trail drive.

Index

Acknowledgements

The publishers would like to thank the following
illustrators for their contributions to this book:

Richard Berridge (Specs Art) 20–21, 22*b*, 23*b*, 24–25, 26–27;
Peter Dennis (Linda Rogers Associates) 4–5, 6, 7*l*, 28–29, 30–31, 32,
33, 34–35; Terry Gabbey (Associated Freelance Artists Ltd) 10–11,
14–15, 16, 18–19, 50–51, 52–53, 56–57*b*; Luigi Galante (Virgil
Pomfret Agency) 36–37, 38–39; Christian Hook 44–45, 46*br*, 47,
48*tr*, 49; John Lawrence (Virgil Pomfret Agency) 58–59, 60–61;
Malcolm McGregor 7*br*, 8, 14*tr*, 15*tr*, 17*l/m*, 21*b*, 23*m*, 40–41, 45*br*,
48*bl*; Tim Slade 4–5*t*, 5*br*, 13, 25*tl*, 28*bl*, 43*t*, 50*bl*, 54–55*t*; Peter
Thoms 25*br*; Shirley Tourret (B L Kearley Ltd) 9*tr/br*, 12, 13*r*,
16–17*t*, 17*r*, 21*t*, 22*tr*, 23*tl*, 25*tr*, 30*tl*, 37*m*,
42*t*, 43*br*, 46*l*, 47*b*, 54–55*b*

Engravings by John Lawrence (Virgil Pomfret Agency)
Decorative border by Mark Peppé (B L Kearley Ltd)

The publishers would also like to thank the following for supplying
photographs for this book:

Amon Carter Museum: 15*tl* *Indian Girls Grinding Corn*
Adam R Vroman; 27*tl* *In Without Knocking* Charles M Russell;
Bridgeman Art Library: 56*tr*; Buffalo Bill Historical Center:
42*bl* *Custer's Last Stand* Edgar S Paxson; J. Allan Cash: 8*t*;
Corbis/Bettman (UK): 25*bl*; 31*t*; 33*tl*; 40*bl* *Buffalo Soldiers* Frederic
Remington; 41*r*; 42*tr*; 56*r*; Empire Interactive: 57*br* Gettysburg;
Ronald Grant Archive: 57*tl*; Kobal Collection: 57*r* & *bl*; Montana
Historical Society: 27*br* *At the Railhead*; Peter Newark's Western
Americana: endpaper *Driving the Golden Spike at Promontory, Utah,
May 10, 1869*; 7*r* *Fall of the Alamo* Robert Onderdonk; 9*tl* *The
Cowboy* Frederic Remington; 33*tl*; 37*bl*; 48*br*; 52*t*; 53*r*; 56*l*, *bl/r*;
Laurence Parent: 39*br*; Southwest Museum: 42–3*b* *The Battle of the
Little Big Horn* Kicking Bear; State Historical Society of North
Dakota: 33*tr* *Pendroy Quilting Party*; Trip/Art Directors: 35*tr*;

and Fort Laramie for their kind assistance.